Beneficiary Directory™

ONE FILE. ONE LOCATION. ONE CALL.™

*Your Personal System
to Organize Your
Important Documents and
Guide Your Beneficiaries*

People Who Are Using the
Beneficiary Directory Recommend It . . .

The *Beneficiary Directory* enables us to provide turn-key information and instructions to our loved ones for when they need it most. It will be hard enough on them when we pass; the *Beneficiary Directory* eliminates the guesswork while settling our affairs. An estate plan is simply not complete without it.

BRETT AND LARISSA NIGRO

After hearing of difficulties people incurred in the area of document availability, we did this for the convenience of our children. As it turns out, it has proven to be a convenience to us. Everything we could ever need in the line of important documents can be quickly located.

JIM AND ALYCE MARTIN

I consider the *Beneficiary Directory* a great gift to my family. At a time of emotional stress, the knowledge that they have to contact only one person to learn the location of all essential papers will bring relief to them and affords me peace of mind now.

DORIS DOULL

It's a relief to know that my loved ones will be able to find my paperwork easily if the need arises. I also appreciate knowing there's a back-up copy of all my important paperwork for my own use.

HANNAH SUKONICK

Simple . . . logical . . . practical . . . functional. Why doesn't everyone have this kind of resource? When faced with my own mortality a dozen years ago, I sought a source to help shelter my wife and children in my absence. The *Beneficiary Directory* brings the financial planning process full circle.

LEN KAGNO

We all have very busy lifestyles . . . if something happens to us, our survivors will have a difficult time getting the papers they need. The *Beneficiary Directory* forces everyone to get his or her life in order. The major benefit of the *Beneficiary Directory* system is that once all the hard work is done . . . we can breathe a bit easier.

WALTER B. EINSTEIN

The *Beneficiary Directory* is such a great idea. It's very easy to understand and follow. We feel better knowing all our important documents will be easy to find in the event that something happens. It's something everyone needs to think about.

RICHARD AND LORI EBBS

...And Industry Leaders Endorse
the *Beneficiary Directory* ...

A useful tool for every family: a great addition to everyone's estate plan. We will all need this information sooner or later.

DAN CANDURA
Certified Financial Planner® Professional

Mark Kaizerman has mastered his field and been providing superior financial guidance to his clients and mine for nearly twenty years. He demonstrates maturity of judgment and understanding of the complex, personal issues which inevitably play such an important part in the implementation of a sound financial program.

JAY J. LANDER, ESQ.
Lander & Lander, P.C., Attorneys at Law

. . . Required reading for anyone concerned about the disposition of their estate. Whether you're a skilled advisor serving your clients, or a consumer trying to put your personal affairs in order, the *Beneficiary Directory* will provide valuable assistance.

DAVID J. KAUFMAN
Certified Financial Planner® Professional
Chartered Financial Consultant

The *Beneficiary Directory* solves one of the biggest issues facing individuals and advisors, namely how to organize and most effectively provide for the intergenerational transfer of information and wealth. This comprehensive yet easy-to-follow book is a must-read for all who want to simplify their lives and best provide for their loved ones.

RICHARD D. SINCERE
President
Sincere & Co., LLC

Families are in a real mess when they don't know where to turn after the death of a parent or spouse.
It is so important to use a directory such as this and have it available at the right time. The *Beneficiary Directory* is complete and thoughtful.

CHRIS HENNESSEY
Faculty Director
Babson School of Executive Education

Beneficiary Directory™

ONE FILE. ONE LOCATION. ONE CALL.™

*Your Personal System
to Organize Your
Important Documents and
Guide Your Beneficiaries*

Mark H. Kaizerman

CERTIFIED PUBLIC ACCOUNTANT
CERTIFIED FINANCIAL PLANNER® PROFESSIONAL

JUST WRITE BOOKS
LOS ANGELES, CALIFORNIA

Just Write Books
Los Angeles, California
www.JustWriteNow.com

For more information on this book, contact the author:
Telephone (508) 647-0830
Fax (508) 647-0845
E-mail info@beneficiarydirectory.com

Designed by Robert Mott & Associates, Mottopia.com

ISBN: 0-9749830-3-9

Trademarks
Beneficiary Directory and *One File, One Location, One Call* are terms
trademarked by Mark H. Kaizerman.

This publication is designed to provide accurate and authoritative information in
regard to the subject matter covered. It is provided with the understanding that
neither the author nor the publisher are engaged in rendering legal, accounting, or
other professional services. As each individual situation is unique, questions
relevant to personal finance and specific to an individual should be addressed to an
appropriate professional to ensure that the situation has been evaluated carefully
and appropriately. The author and publisher specifically disclaim any liability, loss,
or risk which is incurred as a consequence, directly or indirectly, of the use and
application of any of the contents of this work.

For my dad, A. Manuel Kaizerman

Contents

Preface

In October 2003, my dad's physician advised him, "Mr. Kaizerman, it's time to put your life in order." Suffering the effects of pancreatic cancer, Dad was given only three to six months to live. As you can imagine, our family went through all sorts of emotions, but eventually Dad turned to me and said the time had indeed arrived to put things in order.

As a financial advisor, I already knew much of what that would mean. I went through all the files, locating titles to automobiles, identifying bank and investment accounts, and so on. As I did this with my dad's guidance, we decided it was also a good time to throw away the stuff that wasn't needed, like old tax returns and receipts going back twenty or thirty years.

In one drawer, I found Dad's military discharge paperwork from the 1940s, and I was ready to toss it when he said it was an important document I should save. I thought, *It's been almost sixty years since he completed his service. Why would anyone need to see his discharge paperwork?* But, oh well, it was only one more sheet of paper, and obviously it still meant a lot to my father, so I kept it.

Dad's battle with cancer came to an end in April 2004. My brother and I went to the mortuary to arrange for his burial. In planning the memorial service, the funeral director asked the typical questions, but one took us by surprise: He asked if our dad was a veteran. We replied yes, and he informed us that the federal government provides a complimentary U.S. flag for the coffin of all veterans. Our dad had always been very patriotic, and we knew that this would be important to him.

Only one thing we need, the funeral director advised us: Some information that is on your father's military discharge paperwork. Did we know where it was? We smiled. Dad had made sure we would know where to find that information. We were so grateful that our dad got his stars and stripes.

Together, Dad and I created the first beneficiary directory, and it worked. Since then, I have developed additional tools for helping people and their advisors create a fully integrated, personal system for putting their own lives in order. For our family, the important form was military discharge paperwork; with someone else it may be an IRA beneficiary designation form, a marriage certificate, or life insurance policy. The Beneficiary Directory™ is your personal system to organize important documents and guide your beneficiaries. On behalf of your beneficiaries, I thank you.

| # The Challenge . . . The Answer

Many books have been written about financial planning, addressing concerns in the areas of education, retirement, risk management, tax, and estate planning. Most discuss how to handle assets in the event of disability or death, but the Beneficiary Directory is the only system I've seen that shows you how to organize your important documents and guide your beneficiaries. Yet the Beneficiary Directory is not a substitute for comprehensive financial planning; rather, it is an integral part of your risk management and estate plans.

As a financial advisor, I have seen too many cases where spouses or heirs have had to deal with the overwhelming task of managing a loved one's affairs during emotional upheaval. Unnecessarily, they were confronted with locating critical documents and finding valuable advice while also dealing with the other overwhelming activities of this tumultuous time.

Some documents can be found at the office of an attorney, stockbroker, or insurance agent, while others are "somewhere in the house." Of even greater concern than finding what's been stashed who knows where, though, is the fact that things get missed. Every state in this country has unclaimed property, which includes cash from bank accounts, insurance proceeds, and other items no one has claimed. In the Commonwealth of Massachusetts, where I live, the Secretary of the State annually publishes a list of these things. It's always interesting to review this to see if family or friends' names are included: If you come across someone you know, it's like hitting the jackpot. Of course, the only problem is that before you get the excitement of finding the money, someone had to lose track of it.

I created the Beneficiary Directory to address these shortcomings. It provides a bridge to transfer vital information from one generation to the next and establishes a critical link to an advisor so no assets remain unclaimed, and no one has the unnecessary burden of trying to figure out where important documents may be filed.

The Beneficiary Directory system, along with its FactFinder Checklist and related worksheets, presents a way for individuals to put together a directory-type file on their own. To receive the maximum benefit, it is also necessary that you designate an individual as your Beneficiary Directory Access Administrator. This person will assist you in gathering, regularly reviewing, and maintaining the Beneficiary Directory while you are alive, and will also provide the ultimate service of meeting with your beneficiaries when the time comes.

CHAPTER 2 | # The Value in Your Beneficiary Directory

No doubt you've heard the expression, "Where there's a will, there's a way." Indeed, if you have a will (a legal document that provides for the management and distribution of your assets upon your death), then the Beneficiary Directory will provide the "way." While your will gives instructions to your executor, the Beneficiary Directory delivers a comprehensive file of resources (documents and information) that allows your executor to carry out your wishes in the most efficient, cost-effective, and timely manner. The results assure more prompt transfer to your heirs and the swift closing of the probate process.

In the event of disability, those individuals you've designated in a Health Care Proxy (HCP) or Durable Power of Attorney (DPOA) will also gain value and guidance from your Beneficiary Directory. At a time of personal crisis, the Beneficiary Directory dramatically cuts down on the learning curve and allows holders of HCPs and DPOAs to more rapidly "get up and running" on your behalf.

Initially, you may look at the Beneficiary Directory as valuable only to your heirs, and only at your disability or upon your death. There's no question that the value during these times is enormous, but you achieve many benefits right away, too.

▸ In the process of building your Beneficiary Directory, you will identify important documents that may be missing and will create a plan to obtain them.

▸ You may also identify areas of planning that have been overlooked, such as the omission of a contingent beneficiary designation on a retirement account, or opportunities that you have yet to capture, such as the need to update your will to include a new grandchild.

▸ Your Beneficiary Directory provides a convenient reference for all your important information, consolidated in a single location. Often people keep things in multiple locations, some in files at home, in files at work, in the safe deposit box. Have you ever needed some information from a document whose original was not handy? Your Beneficiary Directory is your ultimate reference tool, allowing quick and easy access.

▸ In this post–September 11th era, the importance and value of maintaining back-up copies of your most important documents cannot be over-emphasized. Computer users have long recognized the need to back up their data so nothing gets lost;

in the same way, your Beneficiary Directory is an important part of safeguarding your most important documents.

▸ Let's face it: We have all used our own personal filing system for years, one that works for us, regardless of what others may think. The Beneficiary Directory uses a special Document Key, which is designed to allow you the convenience of continuing to use your filing system, yet unlocks the whole thing for someone else's use when the need arises.

▸ You will gain a skilled and respected personal advisor for you and your beneficiaries, so that in a moment of crisis, an important link to advice (that first call) is clear and in place. This advisor, who is referred to as your Access Administrator, will work with your beneficiaries to ensure that your influence and values are communicated to your heirs.

▸ You will have peace of mind in knowing that you have taken steps toward "Putting Your Life In Order" ("PYLIO" for short, pronounced *pie-leo*) and have provided assistance to a spouse, child, or other beneficiary. Many have found completing their Beneficiary Directory to be a reflective and gratifying process.

▸ Your Beneficiary Directory provides a system for regular review and update of its contents, so that the value in establishing this file continues in the future.

3 | # Beneficiary Directory, An Overview

T he Beneficiary Directory consists of three proprietary and innovative tools that work together to help you achieve its maximum benefits. These tools include the FactFinder Checklist, the Document Key, and the Access List.

▸ **The FactFinder Checklist** provides a detailed listing of documents that may be appropriate for your Beneficiary Directory, allowing you to easily identify and assemble the items you decide to include. It also prompts you to identify missing documents, so that you may obtain them well in advance of any future need.

▸ **The Document Key** serves to unlock your personal filing system, as it cross-references the copies of documents you have placed in your Beneficiary Directory to the location of the originals. The unique design of the Document Key allows you to continue using your own personal filing system without change, yet be assured that your beneficiaries will know where to look for any originals when they're needed.

▶ **The Access List** (or "A-list" for short) contains the names of individual(s) you authorize to have access to your Beneficiary Directory contents. For each individual you include, you'll also select an access code. This allows you to indicate under what circumstances each individual may have access, such as your disability or death.

On the A-list, you will also designate your Access Administrator. The selection of an appropriate person for this role is critical to your success with the Beneficiary Directory. (Later on, you'll learn the criteria for selecting your Access Administrator.)

The contents of your completed Beneficiary Directory file should be kept by your Access Administrator, thus safeguarding valuable off-site copies of your most important documents. And to make certain your Beneficiary Directory always contains the most up-to-date information, you and your Access Administrator should plan an annual review meeting to update its contents.

Most important, in a time of need, you will have provided a valuable link for your beneficiaries to your chosen Access Administrator. He or she will meet with your beneficiary to assist in reviewing and using the contents of your Beneficiary Directory, recommending an action plan that will provide needed assistance with paperwork and other issues.

Imagine: One call means individuals you've authorized on your A-list will have access to the contents of your Beneficiary Directory, know the exact location of valuable original documents, and have the benefit of professional guidance in how best to use what you have created.

Before you go any further . . .

Start by selecting a receptacle for all your documents: an accordion file, a binder, a manila envelope or some other holder you'd like to use. It doesn't have to be fancy, just functional. Your completed Beneficiary Directory will consist of a collection of document copies and other items, so visit your local office supply store and purchase this before going on to the next step.

CHAPTER 4 | # Your FactFinder Checklist

The first tool for building your Beneficiary Directory is the FactFinder Checklist. Your FactFinder Checklist will help you identify the items to be assembled into your Beneficiary Directory, as well as serve as a visual reminder of where you stand in the document collection process. To make it easy to use, the FactFinder Checklist is divided into item sections: Insurance, Savings/Investments, Property, Retirement Plan, Estate Planning, and Personal Data.

You'll find a blank FactFinder Checklist for your own use among the appendices in the back of this book.

STEP ONE

Review each section and place a checkmark next to those items that should be included in your Beneficiary Directory. Don't worry about locating any documents at first; just check all items that apply to you.

Your FactFinder Checklist includes two reports that require you to fill in personal information. These reports are the Savings/Investment Locator and the List of Important Advisors/Contacts.

The Savings/Investment Locator has been designed to summarize information on your bank accounts, investment/brokerage accounts, and safe deposit box(es). The report has four columns, but for now you will be entering information in only three: name, location, and account number. (You will enter information in the right hand column, labeled "Document Key Code," later.) For each bank or investment/brokerage account, enter the bank or custodian name, physical location of bank/custodian, and account number. For your safe deposit box, enter the custodian name, physical location of the custodian, and box number.

The List of Important Advisors/Contacts includes information that may be critical to your beneficiaries. You are prompted to enter contact data for your Access Administrator, financial advisor, attorney, accountant, insurance agent, physician, and employer. The "other" spots are included for you to enter additional contacts who may be appropriate for you. For each contact, enter complete data including full name, mailing address, telephone, fax, and e-mail information.

STEP TWO

Once you have completed checking items on the FactFinder Checklist and filling out the two reports, you are ready to start assembling the documents. This step can take a little more time, and it's important that you carefully follow the next steps. (Note: The more difficult you find the accumulation of your documents, the more apparent the value of the Beneficiary Directory to your heirs. Imagine the frustration your beneficiaries would feel if they were trying to locate these documents in a crisis!)

Review your list and circle the checkmarks you made for any items whose location is unknown. You'll look for these later.

Next, start pulling together the items you have checked but not circled. (Remember, original documents do not go in your Beneficiary Directory, so you should make photocopies. After copying a document, be sure to put the original back where you like to keep it.) Take the copies you have assembled and put them into your Beneficiary Directory file.

Once you add the copy of a document, go back to the checkmark next to it on the FactFinder Checklist and draw a line through the checkmark. Eventually, all the items you have checked on your FactFinder Checklist will either have a line drawn through the check, indicating you have included it in your Beneficiary Directory, or a circle around the checkmark, indicating you do not have or cannot locate the document.

FactFinder Checklist Notations

 Selected for inclusion in your Beneficiary Directory

 Selected, and a copy has been placed in your Beneficiary Directory

Selected, but original can not be located, additional follow-up required

Selected, original could not be located, but now has been obtained, and a copy has been placed in your Beneficiary Directory

Caution: Do not wait until you have assembled all the needed documents before adding copies to your Beneficiary Directory. Add photocopies of the documents as you obtain them.

STEP THREE

Once you've gathered all the documents you can easily locate, it is time to deal with any of those you circled earlier because you didn't know where to look or couldn't find them. You might need to contact a municipal office, insurance agent, attorney, or other individual to request an original. Depending on the type of item and when it was originally generated, you may find it a quick call and you're done, or it could be a process of contacting a series of several different people. Rarely will you find that the trail dead ends before you actually get to someone who can help you obtain a new original.

You may wonder how important each of these documents will be to your beneficiaries. This is where your Access Administrator can be of enormous help, assisting you in sifting the critical from the unnecessary. Each person's situation calls for a unique collection of documents, and a professional advisor will help you determine exactly what you need. This individual, who will serve as an advisor to both you and your beneficiaries, should be involved in all stages of creating your Beneficiary Directory, including a review of your FactFinder Checklist.

An example of a completed FactFinder Checklist, along with the reports, is included on the next page for your reference. Notice how various notations (checkmarks, circles and cross-checkmarks) on the FactFinder Checklist can be used to evaluate your progress in assembling document copies.

Beneficiary Directory™
ONE FILE. ONE LOCATION. ONE CALL.™

FactFinder Checklist

The following are examples of what may be included in your *Beneficiary Directory.* Place a checkmark ✓ next to those items that should be included. If you are unable to locate an item you have checked, then circle the check. (✓) Finally, draw a line through the check to make an X when a photocopy of the item has been placed in your *Beneficiary Directory* ✗.

INSURANCE

Declaration/coverage page(s) of :
- ✗ Medical and dental insurance
- ✗ Health/dental insurance membership cards
- ✓ Life insurance
- ✗ Disability insurance
- ❑ Long-term care insurance
- ✓ Home owner's/renter's insurance
- ✓ Auto insurance
- ❑ Umbrella liability insurance
- ❑ Other insurance policies
- ❑ Appraisals

SAVINGS/INVESTMENTS

- ❑ List/copies of savings bonds, stock and bond certificates in your possession

(Continued on next page.)

SAMPLE : FactFinder Checklist *(Continued)*

☑ Complete **Savings/Investment Locator** for:
- ☑ Bank accounts
- ☑ Investment accounts
- ☑ Safe deposit box
- ☑ Safe deposit key

PROPERTY

- ❑ Business buy-sell agreement(s)

Copies of deed/titles for:
- ☑ Home(s)
- ☑ Automobile(s)
- ❑ Other real property
- ❑ Mortgage/loan information and/or discharge paperwork
- ❑ Auto lease agreement

RETIREMENT PLAN

Primary and contingent beneficiary designation forms for:
- ☑ IRAs
- ❑ Retirement plans (401K, 403B, SEP, etc.)
- ❑ Annuities
- ❑ Life insurance policies
- ❑ Other employer-provided benefit programs

SAMPLE: **FactFinder Checklist** *(Continued)*

ESTATE PLANNING

- ☑ Will(s)
- ☑ Durable power(s) of attorney
- ❑ Health care proxies
- ❑ Trust document(s)
- ❑ Letter of specific bequests
- ❑ Ethical will
- ❑ Divorce agreement
- ❑ Prenuptial agreement

PERSONAL DATA ITEMS

- ❑ Adoption agreement
- ❑ Citizenship papers
- ☑ Passport
- ☑ Birth certificate
- ☑ Social Security card
- ❑ Marriage license
- ☑ Complete **List of Important Advisors/Contacts**
- ❑ Critical medical information and/or summary of family medical history
- ❑ Cemetery plot deed/information
- ❑ Funeral/burial instructions
- ❑ Military discharge paperwork
- ❑ Organ donor card
- ❑ _____

Date Completed: *8/20/04*

SAMPLE

Beneficiary Directory™
ONE FILE. ONE LOCATION. ONE CALL™

Savings/Investments Locator

Record the custodian name, location, and account/box number first. (The Document Key code which will detail the location of your most recent account statements or safe deposit keys will be added later.)

BANK AND INVESTMENT/BROKERAGE ACCOUNTS

Bank/Custodian Name	Location	Account Number	Document Key Code
University Capital & Cash	1 Washington St., Anytown, USA	9921ABX12-0	B
Best Bank Plus	152 Elm St., Anytown, USA	1672D31	B
Quick Brokerage Firm	1987 Riches Ave., Anytown, USA	AYE 1526453	B
Mutual Fund Family A	625 Common St., Anytown, USA	A00176345YW	B

SAFE DEPOSIT BOX(ES)

Custodian Name	Location	Box Number	Document Key Code
University Capital & Cash	1 Washington St., Anytown, USA	1773	C

Date Completed: 8/20/04

SAMPLE

Beneficiary Directory™
ONE FILE. ONE LOCATION. ONE CALL.™

List of Important Advisors/Contacts

Access Administrator and Location of Beneficiary Directory

NAME: Robert Jay, CFP®

ADDRESS: 175 Washington Street, Suite 109

CITY/STATE/ZIP: Anytown, MA 00120

TEL: 123-ABC-1232   FAX: 123-ABC-1233

E-MAIL: roberjay@rj.ysd

Financial Advisor

NAME: Robert Jay, CFP®

ADDRESS: 175 Washington Street, Suite 109

CITY/STATE/ZIP: Anytown, MA 00120

TEL: 123-ABC-1232   FAX: 123-ABC-1233

E-MAIL: roberjay@rj.ysd

Attorney

NAME: M. Grace LaSorsa, Esq.

ADDRESS: 52 Court Street, Suite 1

CITY/STATE/ZIP: Anytown, USA 00120

TEL: 123-ABC-1255   FAX: 123-ABC-1455

E-MAIL: the_law@123.cqt

Accountant

NAME: Meghan Francis, CPA

ADDRESS: 2004 Babo Park

CITY/STATE/ZIP: Anytown, USA 00120

TEL: 123-ASW-7008   FAX: 123-AHC-1165

E-MAIL: Meghan@wtr.yus

SAMPLE: List of Important Contacts *(Continued)*

Physician

NAME: Dr. A. M. Almika

ADDRESS: 75 Madison Avenue

CITY/STATE/ZIP: Anytown, USA 00120

TEL: 123-FTE-9981   FAX: 123-FEW-8817

E-MAIL: almika@hospital.cqp

Employer

NAME: Rosilyn G. Berg, Human Resources

ADDRESS: Widget Factory USA

CITY/STATE/ZIP: Anytown, USA 00120

TEL: 123-4WI-DGET   FAX: 123-FEW-8817

E-MAIL: berg@widget.fac

Other

NAME:

ADDRESS:

CITY/STATE/ZIP:

TEL: FAX:

E-MAIL:

Other

NAME:

ADDRESS:

CITY/STATE/ZIP:

TEL: FAX:

E-MAIL:

Date Completed: 8/20/04

CHAPTER 5 | Your
Document Key

There are many ways to organize (and I use the word loosely) your important financial documents. They include the use of a safe deposit box, fireproof file cabinets, the "blue bag on the office floor" and even "in the pile of stuff next to my desk." An advantage of the Beneficiary Directory is that it does not require you to make any changes in your personal filing system. Whatever you use works for you, and the goal of the Beneficiary Directory is to build on that system. (That is assuming you are pleased with your personal filing system; if you want to change it, that is another area where your Access Administrator can help.)

The Document Key helps to unlock your personal filing system. It has two columns, the Key Code on the left, which lists the letters from A through G, and the Physical Location of Original Documents on the right, which provides a blank space that requires you to make an entry.

Although people often keep original documents in more than one location, papers tend to flock together. For example, some may be in the safe deposit box, others in the bottom drawer of a file in the office, and the balance in a top dresser drawer in the bedroom. Take a look at your assembled documents: Do you see some commonality in the location of the originals?

Using the above as an example for completing the Document Key, next to the letter A in the Key Code column, you would write "safe deposit box" under the Physical Location of Original Documents. Next to B, you would write "bottom drawer of the file next to my office desk." Finally, next to C, you would enter "top dresser drawer in my bedroom."

STEP ONE

Complete the Document Key by describing a physical location next to each letter, A through G. You may find that you don't need to use all of these, which is fine. If you find that your important financial documents are in more than seven locations, however, it may be time to consolidate your filing system. Until you have a chance to do this, go ahead and write in additional locator codes and descriptions.

STEP TWO

Now go back to the document copies you have assembled, and in the lower right corner of each document copy, write the Key Code letter (A, B, C . . .) that corresponds to the location of the original document. Do this for each document copy to be included in your Beneficiary Directory.

STEP THREE

Review your Savings/Investments Locator. Next to each Bank and Investment/Brokerage Account entry that you have made, in the far right column, enter a Document Key Code letter that describes the location of that account's most recent statement. Or, in the case of a safe deposit box, enter the Key Code that describes the safe deposit box key's location. (For reference, you can also see the example on page 19.)

You may find you omitted a location when you first assigned your Key Codes; if so, go back and add it, and then write the corresponding letter on each document copy.

When you are complete, each document copy in your Beneficiary Directory will have a Key Code in the lower right corner that corresponds to a physical location of your original document entry, which is clearly explained in your Document Key. Your completed Document Key unlocks your personal filing system.

Beneficiary Directory™
ONE FILE. ONE LOCATION. ONE CALL.™

Document Key

Key Code	Physical Location of Original Document
A	Safe Deposit Box #1773, located at
	University Capital & Cash (Anytown Branch)
B	Bottom drawer of file next
	to my office desk
C	Top dresser drawer in my bedroom
D	
E	
F	
G	

Date Completed: 8/20/04

6 | Your Access List

At this point, you have reviewed your FactFinder Checklist, started to assemble copies of the documents you wish to include in your Beneficiary Directory, and created your Document Key. Now that you have built your Beneficiary Directory, you must decide who should have access. The Access List (or "A-list" for short) designates those individuals who will be allowed to use your Beneficiary Directory. By assigning each an Access Code, you restrict or open up the files according to your desires. You also indicate who you have selected as your Access Administrator on the A-list.

You will notice that the list prompts you to include the identities and telephone numbers of several individuals, such as the executor, contingent executor, and holders of your Durable Power of Attorney (DPOA) and Health Care Proxy (HCP). You may also want to list children, relatives, or friends. Keep in mind the people listed here should be limited to those who would need to know the information in your Beneficiary Directory, not everyone under the sun. In fact, if you complete the four prompted entries of executor, contingent executor, DPOA, and HCP, you probably have things covered. The A-list is an example of less being best.

Here are some examples of how to use the Access Code. For your executor and contingent executor, you would want to grant access at your death, so next to their names, circle the DE code. If you want to allow them access at medical disability also, circle DI, too. If you want to give them open access anytime, you circle the O.

A word of caution: Be very selective in granting the O (open access anytime). Doing so could result in information being shared with an individual well before it is necessary.

Also, try to limit your use of the P code and your creative urge to make up your own Access Code in the blank space provided. Although you may have no secrets to keep from your children or executors, your Beneficiary Directory will include a lot of personal information—information that is confidential, so limiting access to times of medical disability (DI) and death (DE) probably makes the most sense.

For the A-list to work, you need someone to serve as the Access Administrator. After all, if you are disabled or worse, someone has to be the main point of contact for your Beneficiary Directory. The role of this administrator is to grant access to your Beneficiary Directory based on what you've designated on your A-list, subject to the Access Code, and to physically possess the contents of your Beneficiary Directory.

While the role of the Access Administrator may be filled by anyone, there are several things you should consider in making this selection.

Your Access Administrator should be able to store your Beneficiary Directory in a safe and secure location, not in your home or your office. A goal of the Beneficiary Directory is to provide a back-up file of your most important documents. As I have said, in this post–September 11th era, the importance of off-site back-up files cannot be overstated.

In addition, your Access Administrator should be someone who can be helpful to you in compiling the Beneficiary Directory. For example, in reviewing the FactFinder Checklist, you may not be familiar with several of the documents listed, such as the Durable Power of Attorney. Or you may not fully understand the advantages of obtaining some of the documents, such as an Ethical Will, or you may be missing documents and need an original, but don't know where to turn.

Your completed FactFinder Checklist and Beneficiary Directory contents can be used as a diagnostic tool to evaluate, among other things, the adequacy of insurance coverage and estate planning documents, as well as the appropriateness of your beneficiary designations. It is ideal if your Access Administrator has the talent and knowledge to explain and assist in these areas.

Your Access Administrator will have the responsibility to meet with your beneficiaries at the appropriate time. It is recommended that the individual you select be skilled in advising individuals. He or she should be able to assist your beneficiaries in using the items in your Beneficiary Directory, file necessary paperwork, and offer direction.

The Access Administrator should help facilitate your periodic review of your Beneficiary Directory contents, making sure it is current.

When you review all these considerations, I think it is apparent that the individual best suited to serve as your Access Administrator will be a trusted and respected financial advisor, attorney, or accountant. Whoever you select, make sure he or she recognizes how important this role is in the process—and by all means introduce both your ultimate beneficiaries and individuals listed on your A-list to your Access Administrator.

Beneficiary Directory™
ONE FILE. ONE LOCATION. ONE CALL.™

Access List

ACCESS CODES

O = open access anytime
DI = access only at medical disability
DE = access only upon death
P = specific approval required
      by _____
___ = _____

INDIVIDUAL/ENTITY NAME		ACCESS CODE (circle)
EXECUTOR	Andrew I. Executory	O DI (DE) P ___
	TEL: 123-AYT-4523	
CONTINGENT EXECUTOR(S)	Andrea Planto	O DI (DE) P ___
	TEL: 123-PWJ-4582	
DPOA	Andrew I. Executory	O (DI) DE P ___
	TEL: 123-HYA-6819	
HCP	Barney Haskell	O (DI) DE P ___
	TEL: 123-KCW-6678	
OTHER		O DI DE P ___
	TEL:	
OTHER		O DI DE P ___
	TEL:	

SAMPLE: Access List *(Continued)*

I/we designate <u>Robert Jay, CFP</u> to serve as our Access Administrator. My/our Access Administrator shall grant full access to the contents of my/our Beneficiary Directory to the above individual(s)/entity subject to the Access Code.

Signature(s): *John Dee*   *Loni Dee*

Name(s):   John Dee   Loni Dee

Date(s):   8/20/04   8/20/04

CHAPTER 7 | Closing
Comments

Congratulations! You have completed your Beneficiary Directory. The copies of your most important documents are in a single file, safely stored off-site; your Document Key unlocks your personal filing system; and your A-list and Access Administrator bridge the transfer of information in your Beneficiary Directory from you to your beneficiaries.

Here's a review and several reminders to get the most out of your Beneficiary Directory:

▸ Once a year, conduct a review meeting to update your Beneficiary Directory, including the copies of documents, FactFinder Checklist, Document Key, and A-list. Maybe you bought a new car (a copy of the new car title should be included), or maybe you changed banks or got a new safe deposit box. Many things can happen during a year that may require you to update your Beneficiary Directory. Schedule an annual Beneficiary Directory review meeting with your Access Administrator.

▶ Want to go digital? Scan your entire Beneficiary Directory contents and store the files on a CD. Be sure to scan your marked-up FactFinder Checklist, Document Key, and A-list. It is important that you date your CD, indicating a current "as of" date. Update annually following your review meeting, burning a new CD with a new "as of" date, and then destroy the old CD.

▶ Remember that your Beneficiary Directory, while well-thought-out and well-intentioned, is just a collection of information—important information that your beneficiaries will need. The selection of an Access Administrator is required to make this system work. This person should be involved from the start with your Beneficiary Directory and will serve as a critical member of your advisory team.

Recommendations

Like most things of value in life, your Beneficiary Directory will require diligence from both you and your Access Administrator to complete and maintain. Look into the eyes of your spouse, children, or grandchildren, and you'll realize you really have only one choice: One File, One Location, One Call. You know they deserve it.

You probably know of other people who could benefit from implementing their own Beneficiary Directory. If you have family or friends who would be interested in learning more about the Beneficiary Directory, invite them to visit our website, www.BeneficiaryDirectory.com. You'll find an order form in the back of this book to purchase additional copies.

All of the worksheets are also available, bound together in an easy-to-use 8½" x 11" workbook. Ask your Access Administrator or other trusted advisor about how you can receive a copy for free.

ONE FILE. ONE LOCATION. ONE CALL.

Appendices

BENEFICIARY DIRECTORY FORMS

Summary of Implementation Steps

STEP 1.   Review the entire *Beneficiary Directory* book. Acquire a file or folder to gather your assembled document copies.

STEP 2.   Select an individual to serve as your Access Administrator.

STEP 3.   Review the FactFinder Checklist. Place a checkmark next to those items you decide should be included in your Beneficiary Directory. Complete both the Savings/Investments Locator and List of Important Advisors/Contacts.

Step 4.   Assemble copies of the documents you have checked. (Originals should not be included in your Beneficiary Directory.)

Remember: Do not wait until you have assembled all the needed documents before adding copies to your Beneficiary Directory. Add photocopies of the documents as soon as you have them.

STEP 5.   Circle the checkmarks for items you can't locate.

STEP 6.   Complete the Document Key.

STEP 7.   Complete the Access List.

STEP 8.   Review the FactFinder Checklist items that were circled in Step 4, and determine how to request/obtain the needed document(s).

Step 9.   Inform individuals on your Access List that you are maintaining a Beneficiary Directory, which contains valuable information that will be of assistance to them. Advise those individuals of the name and contact information for your Access Administrator, and under what circumstances they will be granted access to your Beneficiary Directory. It is recommended that you arrange an introductory meeting for your Access List designees and your Access Administrator to review your goals in establishing your Beneficiary Directory.

Step 10.   Periodically review and update all elements of your Beneficiary Directory with your Access Administrator. At a minimum, an annual review and update is recommended.

FactFinder Checklist

The following are examples of what may be included in your Beneficiary Directory. Place a checkmark ✓ next to those items that should be included. If you are unable to locate an item you have checked, then circle the check. (✓) Finally, draw a line through the check to make an X when a photocopy of the item has been placed in your Beneficiary Directory ✗ .

INSURANCE

Declaration/coverage page(s) of :
- ❑ Medical and dental insurance
- ❑ Health/dental insurance membership cards
- ❑ Life insurance
- ❑ Disability insurance
- ❑ Long-term care insurance
- ❑ Home owner's/renter's insurance
- ❑ Auto insurance
- ❑ Umbrella liability insurance
- ❑ Other insurance policies
- ❑ Appraisals

SAVINGS/INVESTMENTS

- ❑ List/copies of savings bonds, stock and bond certificates

❑ Complete **Savings/Investment Locator** for:
- ❑ Bank accounts
- ❑ Investment accounts
- ❑ Safe deposit box
- ❑ Safe deposit key

PROPERTY

❑ Business buy-sell agreement(s)

Copies of deed/titles for:
- ❑ Home(s)
- ❑ Automobile(s)
- ❑ Other real property

❑ Mortgage/loan information and/or discharge paperwork

❑ Auto lease agreement

RETIREMENT PLAN

Primary and contingent beneficiary designation forms for:
- ❑ IRAs
- ❑ Retirement plans (401K, 403B, SEP, etc.)
- ❑ Annuities
- ❑ Life insurance policies
- ❑ Other employer-provided benefit programs

FactFinder Checklist • Page 2 of 3

ESTATE PLANNING

- ❑ Will(s)
- ❑ Durable power(s) of attorney
- ❑ Health care proxies
- ❑ Trust document(s)
- ❑ Letter of specific bequests
- ❑ Ethical will
- ❑ Divorce agreement
- ❑ Prenuptial agreement

PERSONAL DATA

- ❑ Adoption agreement
- ❑ Citizenship papers
- ❑ Passport
- ❑ Birth certificate
- ❑ Social Security card
- ❑ Marriage license
- ❑ Complete **List of Important Advisors/Contacts**
- ❑ Critical medical information and/or summary of family medical history
- ❑ Cemetery plot deed/information
- ❑ Funeral/burial instructions
- ❑ Military discharge paperwork
- ❑ Organ donor card
- ❑ _____
- ❑ _____

Date Completed:_____

Savings/Investments Locator

Record the custodian name, location, and account/box number first. (The Document Key code which will detail the location of your most recent account statements or safe deposit keys will be added later.)

BANK AND INVESTMENT/BROKERAGE ACCOUNTS

Bank/Custodian Name	Location	Account Number	Document Key Code

Savings/Investments Locator • Page 1 of 2

SAFE DEPOSIT BOX(ES)

Custodian Name	Location	Box Number	Document Key Code
_____	_____	_____	_____
	_____		
_____	_____	_____	_____
	_____		
_____	_____	_____	_____
	_____		

Date Completed: _____

List of Important
Advisors/Contacts

Access Administrator

and Location
of Beneficiary
Directory

NAME:

ADDRESS:

CITY/STATE/ZIP:

TEL: FAX:

E-MAIL:

Financial Advisor

NAME:

ADDRESS:

CITY/STATE/ZIP:

TEL: FAX:

E-MAIL:

Attorney

NAME:

ADDRESS:

CITY/STATE/ZIP:

TEL: FAX:

E-MAIL:

Accountant

NAME:

ADDRESS:

CITY/STATE/ZIP:

TEL: FAX:

E-MAIL:

Beneficiary Directory™
ONE FILE. ONE LOCATION. ONE CALL.™

Physician

NAME: _____

ADDRESS: _____

CITY/STATE/ZIP: _____

TEL: _____ FAX: _____

E-MAIL: _____

Employer

NAME: _____

ADDRESS: _____

CITY/STATE/ZIP: _____

TEL: _____ FAX: _____

E-MAIL: _____

Other

NAME: _____

ADDRESS: _____

CITY/STATE/ZIP: _____

TEL: _____ FAX: _____

E-MAIL: _____

Other

NAME: _____

ADDRESS: _____

CITY/STATE/ZIP: _____

TEL: _____ FAX: _____

E-MAIL: _____

Date Completed: _____

List of Important Advisors/Contacts • Page 2 of 2

Document Key

Key Code	Physical Location of Original Document
A	
B	
C	
D	
E	
F	
G	

Date Completed: _____

Access List

ACCESS CODES

O = open access anytime
DI = access only at medical disability
DE = access only upon death
P = specific approval required
    by _____
____ = _____

INDIVIDUAL/ENTITY NAME	ACCESS CODE (circle)
EXECUTOR _____	**O DI DE P** ____
TEL: _____	
CONTINGENT EXECUTOR(S) _____	**O DI DE P** ____
TEL: _____	
DPOA _____	**O DI DE P** ____
TEL: _____	
HCP _____	**O DI DE P** ____
TEL: _____	
OTHER _____	**O DI DE P** ____
TEL: _____	
OTHER _____	**O DI DE P** ____
TEL: _____	

I/we designate _____ to serve as our Access Administrator. My/our Access Administrator shall grant full access to the contents of my/our Beneficiary Directory to the above individual(s)/entity subject to the Access Code.

Signature(s): _____ _____

Name(s): _____ _____

Date(s): _____ _____

Date Completed: _____

Acknowledgements

I would never have completed this book if it weren't for the support and encouragement of the women in my life. To my wife, Michele, thank you for sharing my dreams. To my two angelic daughters, Meghan and Alyx, I could not look with more excitement upon your future. To my mom, Rosilyn, you have provided me so many opportunities, and I am forever grateful.

My ideas could not have taken shape without the skills and talent of Karen Risch, of Just Write Literary & Editorial Partners, whose editing prowess was surpassed only by her patience in dealing with this first-time author. The graphic and design features of this book are the product of Robert Mott, of Robert Mott & Associates, whose creativity is simply amazing.

To my clients whose unique ideas, feedback, and suggestions were so critical to the development of the *Beneficiary Directory,* I say thank you. It is my honor to be of service to such wonderful people.

Finally, to my dad, who taught me so many things: I hope I always bring honor to your memory. *L'Chaim,* "to life!"

About the Author

MARK H. KAIZERMAN, pictured with his father, has been providing financial advice to individuals since 1986. He started his career as a public accountant with a regional firm in Boston, and moved into specializing in financial planning as a member of American Express Financial Advisors' prestigious Gold Team, before founding Kaizerman & Associates in 1994.

Recognized by *Worth* magazine as one the best financial advisors in the country, he has developed a reputation for providing easily understood advice that improves the quality of people's lives. Mark has served as president of the Financial Planning Association (FPA) of Massachusetts, formerly the IAFP.

Mark's credentials include the following licenses or designations: Certified Public Accountant (CPA), Personal Financial Specialist (PFS), Certified Financial Planner® (CFP) professional, Chartered Financial Consultant (ChFC), Certified in Long-Term Care (CLTC), and Registered Investment Advisor (RIA). He is a graduate of the University of Massachusetts, where he majored in accounting, and Babson College, where he earned his MBA.

Mark lives in the Boston area with his family: wife Michele and daughters Meghan and Alyx.

HOW THE LIST WAS CREATED:
Worth's Best Financial Advisors, "The Top Two-Fifty"

"Selecting the Best Advisers from among the many standouts who counsel America's wealthy is no easy task. We start by accepting nominations from readers, industry associations, investment firms, and advisors we know. Candidates are asked to complete an extensive survey detailing their backgrounds, professional designations, client retention rates, and average portfolio returns. We also ask candidates for their best ideas about wealth management and study them carefully. Advisers in the running must submit a sample financial plan and two letters of recommendation. Registered investment advisers must also supply their Form ADV, which describe their services, fee structures, and disciplinary histories (this is a document that any prospective client should review). We verify credentials with industry associations and check backgrounds using the Lexis legal database to search court records.

"Most advisers on our list carry the certified financial planner, or CFP, designation, but it's by no means a requirement. A certified public accountant, or CPA, who is also a personal financial specialist, or PFS, should also be equipped to provide broad-based advice on investments, taxes, and other wealth management issues. Prospective clients, depending on their needs, may want to shop for more specialized credentials. The designations of chartered financial analyst, or CFA, and certified investment management analyst, or CIMA, both suggests expertise in investing and portfolio management.

"All the advisors on our list are taking new clients. Before you sign up, study the fee structures. About 80 percent are fee-only advisers who earn a fixed fee or a percentage of assets under management. The rest accept fees and commissions. If the fit isn't just right, the advisers on our list can provide referrals to other specialists." (*Worth* magazine, July/August 2002, p. 56.)

Order Form

Description	Quantity	Unit Price	Total
Beneficiary Directory		$21.95 ea.	$

Subtotal	$
Tax (MA residents add 5%, $1.10 ea.)	$
Shipping and Handling (Within the Continental U.S., add $4 ea.)	$
Total	$

Billing Address

Please print. To ensure successful processing of your order, please be sure that the billing address you enter matches the billing address of the credit card you're using.

Method of Payment

❑ Check enclosed (payable to Beneficiary Directory)
❑ MasterCard
❑ Visa
❑ American Express

Name as It Appears on Card

Street Address

City   State

Country (if outside U.S.)   Postal Code

Card Number

Expiration Date   Security Code

Shipping Address *(Please provide if different from billing address.)*

The undersigned purchaser certifies that he or she has read and understands all of the terms and conditions on this invoice. All the terms and conditions are part of this sales order, which shall constitute a contract between parties, and there are no expressed or implied warranties, modifications, or performance guarantees other than expressly stated herein.

Cardholder's Signature   Date

Please fax your completed form to (508) 647-0845 or mail with payment to:
Beneficiary Directory
182 West Central Street,
Suite 200
Natick, MA 01760

For orders to be shipped outside the continental United States, bulk orders at quantity discounts, or for more information, please contact us.

Telephone: (508) 647-0830
E-mail: info@BeneficiaryDirectory.com
Website: www.BeneficiaryDirectory.com